A Young Citizen's Guide To:

Central
Government

Richard Tames

HODDER
Wayland

A Young Citizen's Guide series
Parliament
Local Government
The Electoral System
Central Government
The Criminal Justice System
Voluntary Groups
The Media in Politics
The European Union
Money
Political Parties

Published in Great Britain in 2002 by Hodder Wayland,
a division of Hodder Children's Books

Editor: Patience Coster
Series editor: Alex Woolf
Series design: Simon Borrough
Picture research: Glass Onion Pictures
Consultant: Dr Stephen Coleman

British Library Cataloguing in Publication Data
    Tames, Richard, 1946-
    A young citizen's guide to central government
    1. Legislative bodies - Great Britain - Juvenile literature
    2. Great Britain - Politics and government - 1997 - -
    Juvenile literature
    I. Title II. Central government
    328.4'1

ISBN 0 7502 3777 5

Printed and bound in Italy by G. Canale & C.S.p.A., Turin

Hodder Children's Books,
a division of Hodder Headline
Limited, 338 Euston Road,
London NW1 3BH

Picture acknowledgements:
the publisher would like to thank
the following for permission to
reproduce their pictures: Eye
Ubiquitous/Sean Aiden 11; Eye
Ubiquitous /Geof Daniels 4, 13,
16, 27; Impact 25 (John Arthur),
26 (Piers Cavendish);
Popperfoto 5, 8, 17 (top), 22
(top); Popperfoto/Reuter
contents page, 6, 9, 12, 14, 15,
22 (bottom), 24; Press
Association/Topham 17 (bottom),
18, 20, 28, 29; Topham
Picturepoint 7, 21, 23.

Cover: 10 Downing Street
(Impact/Piers Cavendish);
Whitehall, London
(Impact/Simon Shepheard);
Labour Cabinet ministers
(Camerapress/Stewart Mark).

Contents

Central government consists of the Prime Minister, the Cabinet (the chief decision-taking body), junior ministers and the civil service. The Prime Minister is the leader of the majority party in Parliament. The Cabinet and junior ministers are members of Parliament appointed by the Prime Minister. Their function is to govern the country, and protect and promote its interests and well-being. They do this through departments of state, collectively known as the civil service, or by agencies acting for them.

From warfare to welfare A thousand years ago, the main business of government was war. Europe was ruled by kings who fought to defend or extend their lands. By around 1500, strong kingdoms began to develop, notably in England, France and Spain. War was still important for government, but rulers also understood the need to make their countries richer by encouraging trade with other countries and industry at home.

European rulers often called parliaments, or meetings, of representatives of the nobility, Church and towns to gain their advice and assistance in making laws and raising taxes. When co-operation broke down between these groups in seventeenth-century England, it led to civil wars between 1642 and 1649. Parliament and monarch remained partners, but Parliament began increasingly to wield more power. Although Britain's eighteenth-century rulers remained personally involved in appointing ministers, bishops and generals, power shifted into the hands of the Prime Minister and his Cabinet. By the mid-nineteenth century, it was more important for a Prime Minister's government to have the support of Parliament than the approval of the monarch.

10 Downing Street has been the official residence of Britain's Prime Ministers since the 1730s. More than 130 people work in its sixty rooms.

By 1900, the Industrial Revolution had made European countries richer but had also created new problems which governments felt they needed to tackle. These included making cities healthier places to live in, providing schools and regulating working conditions to prevent abuses. With the growth of democracy, governments became answerable to the general public as voters.

A growing government

Over the centuries, central government increased its workload and the number of people it employed. It also increased the amount of national wealth it took through taxes. Over the last twenty years, governments have attempted to reduce the number of people working for them directly while trying to keep up the range and level of services they provide.

In 1938 the government of the United Kingdom employed 581,000 civil servants. But the experience of fighting the Second World War led to much greater government control over people's lives. After the war, the Labour government extended the social security system, created the National Health Service and took over running transport, power and many major industries. Thus, by 1960 the number of civil servants had risen to 996,000. During the 1980s government gave up direct control of many industries and turned tasks over to private businesses – by 1990 the number of civil servants had fallen to 567,000.

'The... object of government is to do for a community of people whatever they need to have done but cannot do at all or cannot do so well for themselves...'
Abraham Lincoln, US President from 1861-65.

The takeover of major industries and services by the Labour government of 1945-51 was known as nationalization. Under the Conservative governments of 1979-97 these industries were returned to private ownership.

THIS COLLIERY IS NOW MANAGED BY THE

NATIONAL COAL BOARD

ON BEHALF OF THE PEOPLE

JANUARY 1 1947

Sharing power

Sharing power Another important change for central government has been a trend towards sharing power with other levels of government. In the UK this means sharing 'upwards' with international organizations, such as the European Union and the North Atlantic Treaty Organization (NATO). The European Union exists to promote trade, investment and co-operation among its members in managing common problems, such as pollution. NATO is a defence alliance of European states with the USA and Canada. Central government also has to share power 'downwards' with the Scottish Parliament and the Welsh and Northern Ireland assemblies. In future, more power may be shared with the government of London and other major cities and possibly even English regional governments.

In 1707, Scotland and England were joined together by the Act of Union, which abolished Scotland's separate parliament. But Scotland kept its own church and systems of law and education. Today's Scottish Parliament also controls such matters as health care but has only limited powers to raise taxes. Matters like defence are still controlled by central government at Westminster in London. The powers of the National Assembly for Wales are also limited and do not include the right to raise local taxes. In Northern Ireland, government is based on sharing power between its Protestant and Catholic communities. The Isle of Man and Channel Islands each have their own parliaments and do not come directly under the control of the Parliament at Westminster.

The Scottish Parliament in session. Devolution – the sharing of power 'downwards' from Westminster – could be the first step towards complete independence for Scotland.

In the United States, the President is both head of state (representing the US on ceremonial occasions) and head of government (responsible for proposing new laws and seeing that existing ones are obeyed). In Britain, these tasks are divided. The Queen is head of state and performs ceremonial duties such as opening Parliament, awarding honours and entertaining foreign heads of state as guests on official visits. The Prime Minister is head of the government and is therefore responsible for running the country.

'The work of a Prime Minister is the loneliest job in the world.'
Stanley Baldwin, Conservative Prime Minister (1923-4, 1924-9 and 1935-7).

No fixed powers

A constitution is the body of rules which sets out how government ought to work. The constitution of the United States lays down clear guidelines for the job of President. In Britain the constitution is largely unwritten and based on law, tradition and practice. The Prime Minister's job is more loosely defined than the role of the American President. What a Prime Minister does largely depends on how they see their job. Clement Attlee (Prime Minister from 1945-51) aimed to get his ministers working together as a team, while Margaret Thatcher (Prime Minister from 1979-90) was more inclined to follow her own strong views and sack ministers who disagreed with her.

Prime Minister Margaret Thatcher and her Cabinet. Thatcher sacked many individual ministers – until 1990, when a majority of Cabinet ministers forced her to resign from office.

Hiring and firing The greatest single source of the Prime Minister's power is patronage – the right to decide who will be in the Cabinet, who will serve as ministers in the government, who will be appointed to hundreds of different boards and bodies, and who will be offered knighthoods and other honours. The Prime Minister is leader of his or her political party, and has the power to appoint, promote and dismiss. Another of the Prime Minister's crucial powers is to decide when a general election will be held, providing it is not more than five years since the previous one.

So much to do The Prime Minister's many tasks include:
- representing Britain at major international meetings (of NATO, the European Union and the Commonwealth);
- chairing meetings of the Cabinet and its key committees;
- overseeing the secret service;
- taking the lead in cases of major national crisis. Prime Minister Tony Blair did this in 1998 to secure the 'Good Friday Agreement' in Northern Ireland, and in 2001 to supervise the campaign to fight an epidemic of foot-and-mouth disease.

Prime Minister John Major visiting British troops during the 1991 Gulf War. Close personal co-operation between the leaders of the US, UK and other allies was essential during this crisis.

The Prime Minister usually meets the Queen once a week to give her a confidential briefing on the work of the government. As leader of a political party, the Prime Minister spends time listening to the views of its members, both in Parliament and out in the constituencies where they are elected. He or she also has to answer the questions of the Leader of the Opposition in Parliament, respond to press criticism, take note of opinion poll findings, and cope with unexpected events as they arise. All this as well as trying to deliver on the package of promises he or she (and his/her party) made to get elected.

The Prime Minister's team

The Prime Minister is supported by a team that has grown steadily in recent years. It includes:
- a Private Office (six people), to co-ordinate relations with various branches of government;
- a Political Office (six people), to handle relations with his or her political party;
- a Press Office (twelve people), to handle relations with the press and broadcast media;
- a Policy Unit (thirteen people), to examine and suggest new programmes and projects;
- a Strategic Communications Unit (six people), to make sure that all ministers follow the Prime Minister's lead in dealing with the media.

There are also advisers, special units and task forces for particular projects or emergencies. The Labour government, elected in 1997, set up four special units, combining government officials and outside experts, to deal with women's issues, the anti-drugs campaign, the efficiency of government and problems of 'social exclusion' resulting from poverty. And Prime Minister Blair has daily contact with his personal Press Secretary, an expert in how government decisions should be put over to the public.

Prime Minister Blair with French Premier Jospin. Regular meetings with other heads of government keep the Prime Minister constantly in the media spotlight.

> **'The main essentials of a successful Prime Minister are sleep and a sense of history.'**
> Harold Wilson, Labour Prime Minister (1964-70 and 1974-6).

So little time... The main practical limit on a Prime Minister's power is simply time. The Prime Minister can chair any Cabinet committee he or she chooses to – but there are not enough hours in the week to chair all of them. There is always too much to do. It is no exaggeration to say that a Prime Minister is at work almost every waking minute. On long journeys the Prime Minister is constantly either reading official papers, listening to advisers or talking by phone. The job is so demanding that personal health and fitness can be key factors in the Prime Minister's political effectiveness. Recent Prime Ministers have found it advisable to appoint a deputy, although the position has no formal standing, unlike that of the Vice-President of the United States.

> **'The politician who never made a mistake never made a decision.'**
> John Major, Conservative Prime Minister 1990-97.

Personal priorities What a Prime Minister chooses to give time to depends at least partly on his or her own past experience and interests. Sir Winston Churchill and Sir Anthony Eden were mainly interested in foreign affairs. Edward Heath was determined that Britain should become a member of the European Union. Margaret Thatcher wanted to reduce the power of trade unions and sell off failing government-controlled industries. Tony Blair's early years in power concentrated on reforming government itself in relation to London, Wales, Scotland and the House of Lords.

British Prime Ministers since 1945

1945-51	Clement Attlee	Labour
1951-55	Sir Winston Churchill	Conservative
1955-57	Sir Anthony Eden	Conservative
1957-63	Harold Macmillan	Conservative
1963-64	Sir Alec Douglas-Home	Conservative
1964-70	Harold Wilson	Labour
1970-74	Edward Heath	Conservative
1974-76	Harold Wilson	Labour
1976-79	James Callaghan	Labour
1979-90	Margaret Thatcher	Conservative
1990-97	John Major	Conservative
1997-	Tony Blair	Labour

The Cabinet is, in effect, the most important committee of central government. In the main it is made up of ministers in charge of major government departments. Some departments always have a minister in the Cabinet. They include:

- the Treasury – this is headed by the Chancellor of the Exchequer. The Treasury controls the nation's taxes and spending. It is such an important department that another of its ministers, the Chief Secretary to the Treasury, is also usually a member of the Cabinet.
- the Foreign and Commonwealth Office – this is headed by the Foreign Secretary. The FCO handles Britain's relations with other countries and international organizations.
- Defence and International Development (the former manages the organization and equipment of Britain's armed forces; the latter handles Britain's aid to poor countries).
- the Home Office – this is headed by the Home Secretary. It deals with internal affairs, including policing, prisons and immigration.

Other government departments represented in the Cabinet usually include Trade and Industry, Health, Environment, Education, Social Security, Rural Affairs, Wales, Scotland, Northern Ireland and the Lord Chancellor, who heads the legal system. One or two ministers may be freed from having to run a major department so that they can support the Prime Minister as 'trouble-shooters', or take over the chairing of key Cabinet committees. These 'ministers without portfolio' may have titles such as Lord Privy Seal or Chancellor of the Duchy of Lancaster.

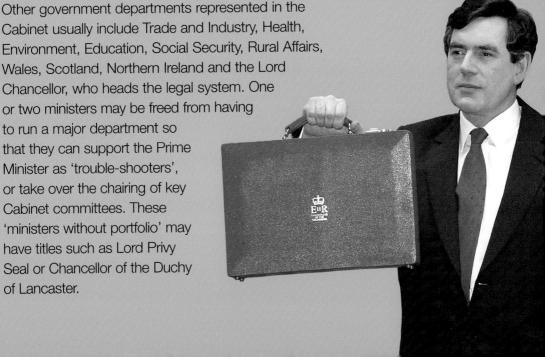

Chancellor of the Exchequer, Gordon Brown, holds the famous despatch box which contains his Budget speech, announcing tax and spending plans.

Meetings

Normally there are just over twenty members in the full Cabinet, which meets in a first-floor room at the back of 10 Downing Street in London, the Prime Minister's official residence. Meetings are confidential and who says what is supposed to remain strictly secret. Over the last half century, effective decision-taking has shifted increasingly from the full Cabinet to its committees. In the 1950s, Cabinets met about one hundred times a year, and each meeting lasted up to three hours. By the 1970s this was down to about sixty times a year – twice a week when Parliament was sitting. By the 1990s it was about forty – and under Tony Blair meetings rarely lasted more than an hour. The Cabinet still decides what laws should be proposed to Parliament, it approves the Budget and it co-ordinates the work of government departments. Lord Wakeham, who served in Cabinet under Prime Ministers Thatcher and Major, suggests that the full Cabinet is now 'a reporting and reviewing body rather than a decision-taker'.

Committees, committees

Until 1992 the number and membership of Cabinet committees were kept secret. In that year it was revealed that there were twenty-six Cabinet

All together – the Labour Cabinet of 1998. All change – members of the Cabinet team may be 'reshuffled' if they fail to perform well or deserve promotion.

'The job of a Prime Minister is to get the general feeling – collect the voices. And then, when everything reasonable has been said, to get on with the job and say: "Well, I think the decision of the Cabinet is this, that or the other. Any objections?" Usually there aren't.'
Clement Attlee, Labour Prime Minister from 1945-51.

committees. These are permanent committees which deal with policy matters, including economic and domestic policy, defence and overseas policy, science and technology, home and social affairs, and legislation. These major committees may in turn create sub-committees to consider specific current problems such as terrorism, drug abuse, refugees etc. Specific committees may be appointed to review newly identified problems or 'hot spots', for example situations in which British forces are serving overseas. Ministerial committees consist of government officials who co-ordinate the work of different ministries so that they work together and not at cross-purposes. The Cabinet Office prepares the agendas of the Cabinet and its committees, records their decisions and follows them up to see that they have been turned into action.

The Prime Minister not only decides on the size of the Cabinet and which ministers will serve in it, he or she also chairs Cabinet meetings, sets the agenda (the list of issues to be raised), sums up discussions and oversees the minutes that record the decisions made. The Prime Minister also decides on the number of Cabinet committees, appoints their chairperson and members and defines what they should deal with.

Collective responsibility In theory, all
Cabinet ministers are bound to defend in public any decision taken by the Cabinet, even if they argued against it before the decision was made. If they feel they cannot be loyal to their Cabinet, they are expected to resign. As ministers are usually unwilling to give up top political jobs, they may often let their opposition to a decision be known indirectly by having it 'leaked' secretly to a journalist by a friend or an assistant.

Cabinet minister Peter Mandelson, a close personal friend of Prime Minister Blair, resigned under pressure from the media for alleged abuses of political power for personal advantage.

The organization of central government changes as its work and priorities change. Two hundred years ago, there were no ministries for education or health because these were not matters with which a government was expected to deal. When Britain was still the head of a worldwide empire, which included a quarter of the world's area and population, there was a separate Colonial Office to manage relations with colonies, such as Jamaica and Nigeria. Later this was merged with the Foreign Office. Separate departments for the armed services – War Office (Army), Admiralty (Royal Navy) and Air Ministry (Royal Air Force) – have gradually been merged into a single Ministry of Defence.

The importance and rank of departments of state may change over time. The Treasury and Home Office have always been regarded as important. Forty years ago, Education was not believed to be important enough for its minister to sit in the Cabinet. Since then, attitudes have changed and, more recently, a new Department of Culture, Media and Sport has also been given Cabinet rank.

Deputy Prime Minister John Prescott, whose responsibilities include transport, visiting the site of a train crash.

Mergers and demotions Ministries may
be merged if it is believed that this will improve
government efficiency. Education was merged
with Employment, then Employment was
transferred to Social Security to create a new
Department of Work and Pensions.

Today, questions affecting the environment, farming,
food supply and life in the countryside are all
thought to be interconnected. This has led to the
creation of a new Ministry of Environment, Food
and Rural Affairs (DEFRA).

The former Ministry of Agriculture, Fisheries and
Food (MAFF) was severely criticized over its
handling of a series of crises about the safety of
eggs, milk and meat. Because of this, its powers to
monitor food quality were passed to an
independent Food Standards Agency. After the
foot-and-mouth disease outbreak of 2001, MAFF
was merged into the new DEFRA.

Prime Minister Harold
Macmillan said that the
hardest thing about the
job was dealing with
events that seemed to
come out of nowhere.
National crises
concerning BSE (below)
and foot-and-mouth
disease are good
examples of such
events.

Apart from the twenty or so ministers who make up the Cabinet, there are usually about a hundred other junior ministers. While Cabinet-rank ministers are called Secretary of State, junior ministers are referred to as Minister of State or Parliamentary Under-Secretary of State. The main task of a junior minister is to support the Cabinet minister who heads his or her department.

A major department A look at the Home Office, a large, old-established government department, illustrates the degree of organization necessary and the number of ministerial responsibilities that are involved in the running of central government. The Home Secretary heads the Home Office, taking responsibility for the overall work of the department, setting its budget, approving senior staff promotions and generally acting as its leading spokesperson in dealing with the media. The Home Secretary also takes personal charge of the most sensitive aspects of the department's work, such as national emergencies, terrorism and the security of the royal family.

The Prison Service Agency is responsible for 'operations' – the day-to-day running of prisons – but the Home Secretary has overall responsibility for policy matters, such as how many prisons there are and what they should be for.

There are three Ministers of State at the Home Office. The most senior minister acts as the Home Secretary's deputy and takes special responsibility for prisons, the probation service, and laws and programmes affecting the ordinary family. Another minister deals with the police force, crime reduction and drugs, while the third covers nationality issues such as immigration, passports and asylum for political refugees.

There are also two Parliamentary Under-Secretaries of State in the Home Office. One of these deals with a wide range of miscellaneous matters, including freedom of information, race relations, data protection, gambling, the sale of alcohol, fire services and animal welfare. The other mainly shares the load with senior ministers on police and prison issues. However, this Parliamentary Under-Secretary of State also has several special concerns, including football hooliganism and relations with the Isle of Man and Channel Islands, which have their own separate parliaments, laws, courts and police forces.

Tackling particular issues such as soccer hooliganism (left) or the flow of asylum-seekers (below) involves co-ordinating different departments and agencies, such as police, law officers, immigration control, education and social security.

A week's work inside Westminster

Ministers work very long hours. Typically they expect to be in or around Westminster on weekdays when Parliament is sitting. When the work of their own department is being discussed in the House of Commons, they are usually present to contribute to the debate or respond to questions. They may also be summoned to answer questions put by a House of Commons committee examining the work of their department. The more senior ministers also have to attend meetings of Cabinet committees, even though they may not be of Cabinet rank themselves.

Ministers of all levels spend much of their day in meetings with civil servants, reviewing the work of their department and planning future programmes and legislation. The planning of legislation involves meeting representatives of groups likely to be affected by it. A change in the criminal law might involve meetings with representatives of the legal profession, police, prison and probation officers and civil liberties organizations.

> **'Ministers exist to tell the civil servant what the public will not stand.'**
> Sir William Harcourt (1827-1904), Liberal politician.

...and outside Ministers may or may not choose to give interviews to journalists. As politicians, they know that personal publicity may help to win them promotion; but they cannot guarantee that the publicity they receive will be favourable.

To get a feel of how their department is doing, ministers must visit organizations that are on the receiving end of the policies for which they are responsible. A minister in charge of cracking down on fake goods, for example, would want to meet

Politicians sometimes try to control the publicity they get by only giving interviews to particular journalists they know well and trust.

local trading standards officers and customs officers, and to wander around markets and boot sales and visit the head offices of genuine manufacturers and honest retailers.

Ministers also benefit from visits overseas to learn from other governments' experiences of dealing with particular issues, or simply to improve co-operation in tackling shared cross-border matters, such as aviation and pollution.

When the long day at the office is finished, a minister may well have to go on to an official reception or dinner. Often there will be more work after that, late into the night, reading official 'red boxes' of reports and letters drafted by civil servants. Except for the few who sit in the House of Lords, ministers remain Members of Parliament and so usually return to their constituencies at weekends to hold regular 'surgeries', to which local voters can bring their problems and complaints. Finally the minister might like to try and find some time to spend with his or her family!

Is it worth it? Ministers receive an extra salary on top of their £48,371 pay as an MP. Although they are entitled to an additional £66,172, in 1997 Labour Cabinet ministers deferred the pay rise that was awarded to them; they took it, however, on re-election in 2001. Considering their long hours and their responsibility for budgets running to billions of pounds, a minister's total salary of £114,543 is less than a tenth of the amount that someone with the same sort of responsibilities could be paid in business. On the other hand, they do have a chance of getting their names in the history books – which most business executives do not.

> **'I say to myself that I mustn't let myself be cut off in there, and yet the moment I enter, my bag is taken out of my hand, I'm pushed in, shepherded, nursed and above all cut off, alone. Whitehall envelops me.'**
> Richard Crossman, Labour minister from 1964-70.

Civil servants are permanent, full-time civilian employees of the central government. The heart of the civil service is in Whitehall, London, where major government departments such as the Treasury and Foreign and Commonwealth Office are located. 'Whitehall' is often used as a shorthand term, meaning the top level of the civil service.

Of the 463,266 civil servants employed by government in 1998, only about five per cent work in central London. At their head are 500 or so high-ranking civil servants, often known as 'mandarins' (a reference to the highly educated officials who ruled the Chinese empire for twenty centuries). The top grade of civil servant is the Permanent Secretary, who is responsible for the overall running of a department, promotion of its staff, preparation of its budget, and advising the minister on various issues. Very large departments may have a Second Permanent Secretary. Others have a Deputy Secretary who is supported by under-secretaries, assistant secretaries, scientific officers and executive officers in a pyramid of power stretching down to administrative assistants.

The grandeur of the older Whitehall ministry buildings is a reminder of the days in which Britain ruled a worldwide empire.

'You don't need brains to be a Minister of Transport because the civil servants have them.'
Ernest Marples, Conservative Transport Minister, 1959-64.

From patronage to selection

In eighteenth-century Britain, most government appointments were given to the friends, relatives or political supporters of the government of the day, rather than to people best qualified by knowledge or experience to do the job. This method of appointment was called 'patronage', and has also been known as the 'spoils system'. Apart from often leading to the appointment of incompetent candidates, it also meant a large-scale turnover of office-holders every time the government changed. This made it difficult for competent office-holders to build up experience and for departments to follow through any particular programmes or projects consistently.

The nineteenth-century novelist Charles Dickens attacked the workings of the government of his day in his novel *Little Dorrit*. In Dickens' book, William Dorrit is ruined by the (fictional) Circumlocution Department, whose officials' constant delays and incompetence make it impossible for him to carry out a government contract and are responsible for him ending up in a debtor's prison, through no fault of his own.

This 1960s photo illustrates the typical and somewhat comical image of civil servants as middle-aged men in bowler hats. Today's civil service actively tries to recruit women and members of ethnic minorities.

At the same time that Dickens was making this attack, the government was putting in place a new system for recruiting officials. The system was amended to ensure that civil servants were selected by examination, not personal recommendation, and were chosen from the very best graduates of the ancient universities of Oxford and Cambridge. They would then serve for some forty years, from their early twenties until retirement in their sixties.

For more than a century this system of recruiting senior civil servants was held to be highly successful. Britain's mandarins were admired for their expert knowledge, honesty and devotion to public service. Their behaviour was often compared with that of civil servants in other countries where the spoils system was still in operation and where bribery and corruption of public officials was commonplace. Scandals involving civil servants were very rare in Britain.

During the Second World War experts were recruited into government as both civil servants and politicians (above) to meet the needs of the emergency.

As government took on additional tasks, the number of civil servants continued to grow, reaching a peak during and just after the Second World War. During the war, an entire new Ministry of Food, with 50,000 staff, was created just to control the nation's food supply. Since that time, however, there has been much criticism of the civil service and there have been constant attempts to change how its members are recruited, paid, promoted and the way in which they work.

Theory and practice In theory, Britain's elected politicians are responsible for making policy and the duty of civil servants is to provide them with impartial advice and to obey their instructions absolutely. In practice, the way in which ministers and mandarins work together is more complicated. Civil servants are lifelong experts on their subject. A health minister may have been a doctor or an education minister may have been a teacher – but that does not make either of them an expert on

Conservative minister Alan Clarke wrote that he believed his officials were filling up his diary with speaking engagements round the country to keep him out of the way.

large-scale budgets or building programmes. Usually ministers have no direct experience of the work of the ministry they are in charge of – and often they will move on to another ministry after a while. Ministers are also outnumbered by their senior civil servants by about 65 to 1. So a minister has to be very strong-minded not to allow civil servants simply to take charge.

One way in which ministers challenge their civil servants about a particular issue is to set up a 'task force', consisting of officials and outside experts, to consider the problem and make specific proposals by a set deadline. By 2001, the Labour government had set up more than 300 task forces. Successful ministers who gain control of their departments (rather than being controlled *by* their departments) agree that it is important to be very clear about what you aim to achieve and be willing to put in long hours to keep on top of mountains of paperwork.

'Every department wages a paper war against its ministers. They try to drown him in paper so that he can't be a nuisance.'
Labour minister Richard Crossman, expressing his fears that civil servants, not politicians, were really in control of policy matters.

The cast of *Yes, Prime Minister,* the follow-up to the successful television series *Yes Minister*, pose on the doorstep of 10 Downing Street.

Yes, Minister
During the 1980s, BBC television broadcast a highly successful comedy series, *Yes, Minister*, which showed how a not very bright politician, Jim Hacker, was constantly outwitted by his chief civil service adviser, Sir Humphrey Appleby. *Yes, Minister* was hugely popular with the public and with politicians, including Prime Minister Margaret Thatcher, and was sold to other countries around the world. From Algeria to India and China audiences agreed: 'Yes, that's how real politics work here, too.'

In the aftermath of the Second World War there began to be a general questioning of the nature of British institutions. Why, commentators wondered, if Britain had been on the winning side at the end of the war, were the defeated powers, Germany and Japan, becoming so much more prosperous than we were? Why were British goods less highly regarded than in the past? Why were there so many strikes disrupting industry, transport and public services? Much of the blame for these things was heaped upon politicians. However, in the 1960s, serious criticism began to be directed towards senior civil servants. They were accused of:

- being drawn from a narrow range of public schools and universities, chiefly Oxford and Cambridge; it was suggested that they were arrogant, and failed to understand the lives of ordinary working people;
- having only a broad general education in subjects such as history, literature or languages and therefore lacking understanding of science, technology and management;
- favouring caution and compromise over change;
- being 'invisible' or 'faceless' and therefore not properly accountable for their actions.

Changes

Since 1988 a number of major changes have been made to the way in which senior civil servants work. Automatic pay rises based on years of service have been replaced by pay levels related to how effective an employee is at his or her job (performance-related pay). It is now possible for the public to identify civil servants responsible for particular programmes through press conferences or web sites. Many ministers appoint their own special policy advisers to provide alternative views to the suggestions and information presented by their civil servants.

Investigations into the political impartiality of civil servants, like those of the 1996 Scott Report (below), have drawn sometimes unwelcome attention to the ways in which civil servants are appointed.

Efforts have been made to recruit and promote future top-level civil servants from a wider social and educational background, and to increase the number of women and candidates from ethnic minorities. But this is a slow process. In the mid-1990s, a quarter of a century after the Oxbridge bias was first criticized, fourteen of the twenty largest Whitehall departments were still run by Oxbridge graduates, sixteen of them by ex-public school pupils. All the departments were run by men, three-quarters of whom had spent their entire career in the civil service.

Margaret Thatcher's government drastically reduced the number of civil servants by transferring their work to executive agencies. There are now over 150 of these, the largest of which is the Benefits Agency, handling £80 billion of social security payments and employing 70,000 staff. Subsequently, John Major's government introduced the Citizen's Charter programme. This required all public services to set targets and standards for measuring their performance, and to publish the results. Today, the chief executives of Customs and Excise, the Prisons' Service and the Benefits Agency are employed on short-term contracts of three to five years, whereas previously these organizations had been run by civil servants with safe jobs for life. Short-term contracts are intended to ensure that work is 'performance driven', in other words that it results in higher standards, greater efficiency and better value for money.

Prime Minister Major launching the Citizen's Charter scheme in 1991. The scheme required public services to offer clear information, choice, courtesy, convenience and value.

Tony Blair's administration has continued to press home the idea that departments of central government should think of the public as 'customers' to whom they are delivering services. A People's Panel of 5,000 citizens has been established to provide public feedback to government policies. Its job is to identify areas of policy in which people think more money should be spent (health, tackling crime, education, and so on) and the areas they are most dissatisfied with (public transport and the state of the roads). The Panel is to be consulted at least three times a year. Another task the government has set itself is to sort out the huge muddle of more than a hundred different overlapping boundaries for regional authorities delivering such services as health, transport or environmental control.

The current emphasis is on 'joined-up government', in other words, closer co-operation between different departments, agencies and outside bodies such as charities or churches when it comes to tackling problems like drugs. It is now acknowledged that social problems such as this require the involvement of specialists in health, education and crime control.

Railways are now run by private companies – but the public still blames the government when services break down.

Quangos Departments of state are headed by ministers who can be questioned directly in Parliament over how they handle their work. However, many important bodies are not departments of state but 'quangos' (quasi-autonomous non-governmental organizations), also known as EGOs (extra-governmental organizations) or NDPBs (non-departmental public bodies). Quangos are run by boards whose members are appointed by the Prime Minister or other senior ministers.

Many quangos have been created because successive Prime Ministers have wanted to 'slim down' central government by separating out tasks that could be done more cheaply or just as easily by an independent organization. Examples of this include licensing motor vehicles or checking for breaches in health and safety regulations at workplaces. Today, hospitals are run by some five hundred NHS trusts, rather than directly by the Department of Health, which concentrates on setting guidelines, standards and targets. Quangos control about a fifth of all government spending. Important quangos include:

- the Arts Council, which funds museums and theatres;
- the Audit Office, which checks up on the finances of central and local government;
- OFSTED, which inspects schools and colleges;
- the Commission for Racial Equality, which ensures that laws against racial discrimination are observed.

'Governments are easily tempted to set up a quango for every problem. Shouldn't people eat fewer chips and more apples? Let's set up a health promotion authority.... Whitehall breathes a collective sigh of relief that a problem has been tackled... a press campaign countered. The quango... creates the impression of doing something.... Quangos should exist only when they can be given clear instructions and a clear purpose....'
John Redwood, Conservative politician.

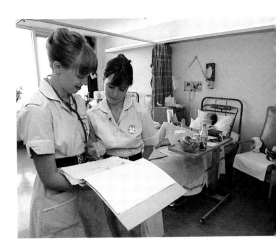

When governments set number targets for hospitals and schools, they inevitably add to the burden of form-filling to show that targets have been met.

Technology Quite apart from the wish of any government to improve public service performance, save money and cut down paperwork, increased efficiency is being driven by the continuing impact of information technology. A computer system has been set up to enable anyone changing their address to notify every relevant government department or agency – local council, health authority, tax office, vehicle licensing etc. – with one single electronic message. By 2005, the government hopes to make it possible for all of its services to be delivered online and all citizens who want it to have internet access.

Checks and balances Governments have great powers to order, tax and regulate the lives of ordinary people. It is therefore essential to monitor the way in which these powers are used. To this end, Parliament holds government to account on a daily basis whenever it is sitting. The Prime Minister and other ministers must defend their actions and provide information at Question Time. The broad outlines of government policy are debated, and committees of MPs question ministers and civil servants and produce reports based on their findings.

The courts, including the European Court of Human Rights, also have an important part to play, especially when ruling whether a minister has acted beyond the powers given by law. The Audit Office checks the spending of taxpayers' money. Civil liberties groups keep a constant watch for abuses of power. All government departments and agencies are required to have complaints procedures. Anyone dissatisfied with the outcome of a complaints enquiry can turn to an MP, who will pass the matter on to the Parliamentary Commissioner for Administration (Ombudsman) to look into.

Keeping in touch – the inspector general of prisons talks to young offenders about their conditions and experiences.

Television, radio and the press provide, in effect, a twenty-four hour, year-round monitoring service on the performance of government. Specialist journalists called lobby correspondents meet MPs daily to exchange gossip. Government policies are analyzed in editorial columns and on letters pages of newspapers. However, the most important check on government is that ordinary people should take an interest in it. With the coming of the internet this has never been easier. You can make a start at http://www.ukonline.gov.uk

Facing the nation – Prime Minister Blair always put high priority on his ability to communicate directly with voters via television.

Activity
Draw up a constitution for a mythical country, or for Britain in the twenty-first century. Would you prefer a constitutional monarchy with a Prime Minister as head of government, or a republican model with a President? Give reasons for your choices. Do you think the Prime Minister is too powerful or too weak in relation to Cabinet and Parliament? How might you restrict or extend his or her powers? What departments of state would you like to see? Do you feel that some issues are under-represented at government level – for example, perhaps you would like to see a minister for young people, or for women, or for ethnic minorities? What sort of people would you choose to draw up a new constitution?

Glossary

accountable having to answer for one's actions

cabinet the main, decision-taking body of central government, consisting of the most important ministers and chaired by the prime minister

cabinet committees permanent committees which deal with matters of policy

cabinet minister a politician who leads a major government department

civil servant a permanent, non-political employee of a government department, responsible for advising ministers and carrying out government decisions

civil service permanent professional branches of state administration

Commonwealth an association of countries which were formerly governed by Britain as part of its empire

constituency an area (average 70,000 voters) which elects a Member of Parliament

democracy a system of government based on free elections in which voters can choose between candidates of varying parties; a free media and legal guarantees of minority rights are safeguards to the working of a democracy

executive agency an organization which carries out a public service under the overall control of government, although it is not directly part of it

junior minister a politician who is appointed to support the cabinet minister who leads his or her department

majority party the party with the most seats in the House of Commons

nationalization government ownership and control of services or industries

parliament the supreme law-making body in the UK

patronage the power to make awards and appointments to jobs

press conference a meeting of journalists from press, radio and television, called to hear an announcement of government policy and ask questions about it

prime minister head of government responsible for running the country

privatization the returning of nationalized companies to private ownership and control

public school traditional, fee-paying, private schools (usually boarding) which have in the past educated most of Britain's senior politicians, civil servants, judges, generals etc.

Question Time a daily session in the House of Commons at which ministers answer questions from MPs about the work of their departments; the Prime Minister takes questions weekly on Wednesdays

treaty an international agreement between governments

trouble-shooter a minister assigned to deal with an issue that is urgent but essentially short-term, such as seeing that the requirements of a new international agreement are met throughout government

Resources

The following national web sites are useful sources of information on central government:

http://www.ukonline.gov.uk this is the official Government Information Service, which links with all government departments and other public bodies

http://www.number-10.gov.uk for 10 Downing Street, and what the Prime Minister is doing

http://www.servicefirst.gov.uk the Cabinet Office site, giving details of such matters as the People's Panel

http://www.europa.eu.int./index-en.htm this site serves the European Union and links with the European Commission, European Parliament and European Court of Justice

Almost every major government department has its own web site, giving details of its organization, services and publications. Major sites include:

http://www.fco.gov.uk the Foreign and Commonwealth Office

http://www.homeoffice.gov.uk the Home Office

A number of universities also have relevant web sites:

http://www.ucl.ac.uk/constitution-unit/ University College, London's unit for keeping up-to-date on changes in the constitution

http://www.psr.keele.ac.uk Keele University's site links with many overseas sites

There are also a number of sites maintained by trustworthy commercial organizations:

http://www.ukpolitics.org.uk gives access to more than 2,500 sites on British politics

http://www.mori.com.polls/ the polling company MORI's site has information about public attitudes to politics and politicians

To search for current and recent political news, try newspaper and broadcasting organizations' sites, such as:

http://www.ft.com the *Financial Times* site, which gives access to over 10 million articles

http://www.guardian.co.uk the *Guardian* newspaper site

http://www.bbc.co.uk the BBC's web site

All the main political parties also have their own web sites.

Visit www.learn.co.uk for more resources.

Index

Numbers in **bold** refer to illustrations.